r a g e.

Amanda Harris

Published by Miscreant Press, 2015
Poems: Amanda Harris
Cover Art: Amanda Harris

"*Thou art not fit to hear thyself convinced;*
Yet should I try, the uncontrollèd worth
Of this pure cause would kindle my rapt spirits
To such a flame of sacred vehemence

That dumb things would be moved to sympathize,
And the brute earth would lend her nerves and shake"

--John Milton (*Comus*)

"*If anything happens to me, make sure people know Chris did it*"

--Nancy Benoit

The following pieces have either been published or are forthcoming in various journals:

Born to Lose (Camroc Press Review)
To My First Crush (Camroc Press Review)
Below Heaven (Camroc Press Review)
PTSD (Camroc Press Review)
Pussy (Black-Listed Magazine)
An Almost Made-Up Story (Negative Suck)
Violence, Interrupted (Negative Suck)
Letter for K (Negative Suck)
Pyromania (Negative Suck)
Break (Negative Suck)
After Prom (Negative Suck)
Abusive Lover (Negative Suck)
Before a Suicide (Negative Suck)
Macy's (MadHat Annual)
Ball and Chain (MadHat Annual)

Table of Contents

An Almost Made-Up Story

It's Monday morning and my teacher is drunk as hell. You can smell the Guinness on his breath, on his clothes. Even the chairs are covered in some kinda stain or another--piss or cum or whatever comes out of a man's body when he's fucked up. You'd think the principal would've put this guy in a sober home, or at least bought air freshener, so that we didn't have to be reminded that our role model was destroying slowly himself every time we walked in his room, but I guess that would be like throwing money down a rabbit hole and expecting no one to jump down there and steal it out of your hands. I mean, don't get me wrong—I love my teacher. He's the guy who showed me everything I know about writing. Still though, when he comes into class like this, it's hard not to wish that he would just go to sleep one day and never wake up. All of my friends tell me I should go easier on the guy—there are divorce papers on his desk and besides, anyone who loses the love of his life has the right to be miserable. And I mean, I've had enough breakups to understand what it feels like—the rage, the shame, the days and days of regret. The problem isn't that I don't want to sympathize. It's that I can't understand why someone who has a good job and a big house and all these kids who want to be like him would need a bottle of Jack Daniel's just to be able to look at himself when he gets undressed at night. I've thought of asking him, of just coming right up to his face and saying that he shouldn't walk around smelling like booze, but I'm afraid that he'll get violent on me, the way all boys get when you insult their manhood. Swearing and hitting, swinging their fists in your face like they want to kill you. My friends say that any guy who needs to push around others just needs to feel like he's better than something. Even so, I wish I could be more forgiving. I wish I could scoop my teacher into a hug, throw out the booze, say out loud that everything will be okay but until he learns to puts his fists down, I avoid him. You never know what a man can do.

Born to Lose

As he pulled out of her driveway, she thought of all of the places he touched her: nipples, breasts, thighs, hips, ass. Wherever she poked smelled like wet shame. For months, she'd been having that fantasy--bang the new teacher—and why not, he was twenty something and single. Every girl in homeroom said some version of the same thing, how easy it would be to get him naked, but the only men they ever tried to get were fifteen-year-old boys with acne and abandonment issues. She needed something bigger and more abusive, the kind of man who lived for bar fights and fists, who didn't need to lie about his age to get her drunk. Sure she was diabetic, sure the vodka he slipped into her orange juice had enough sugar to kill her, or at least make her lose her memory for the night, but maybe that's what you want when someone who's supposed to be your role model strips to his pants, gropes you and calls you his bitch. Maybe that's the only way to get through this ugly thing everyone calls love.

First Hangover

When I was 17, I thought
that if I drank enough beer,

I would turn into a bull.

Every party,
my best friend would

beg me with his wallet-

Have one, Amanda,
just this one,

please, I'll pay you.

One night in high school,
broke, hungry

& learning, too slowly,
to live on nothing,

I drank a fridge's worth
of Budweiser.

Night closed into heartbeats.

Every room I entered
became a container

of impossible things
that opened and

turned inwards.

The next morning,
two men in hospital uniforms3

beat their weight
against my stomach.
I awoke to silence

3

& the failure
of human flesh

Practice

When you yelled *run*, we ran the entire track, each one of us silently praying that the rain and the thick fog would give us something to hate other than our own bodies. I mouthed curse words at you for the two sizes too small T shirt you made us wear. I sucked the air out of my cheeks to make myself look like I had anorexia for more than three days. Mostly though, I imagined you picking us off the field, one by one, until only I was left there, pretending to be lifeless.

Violence Interrupted

Here is the broken thing I am learning to love,
here is the mouth that says nothing.

I wanted a god shaped from iron,
but here you are, straw, blood and bone,

my dirty-haired rascal, wrestling
shadows in a football field.

Last night, found you unconscious in a ditch,
unstitched sweatshirt, cracked bottles for pillows.

All of your old words felt inadequate,
so I coaxed new sounds from dead fists.

My fingers spoke of chest compressions,
of 1, 2 counts and lips that never stopped shaking.

In the language of *breath*, the only certainty is that
at some point, anything will want its body back.

Here is where you say you are only loveable broken.
Here are all the places I mouthed *yes,* then *no*, then *yes.*

One Night Stand

Sometimes, I think I was born to suffer, that it's in my genes to hit on guys who grab my ass and leave me crying in a bathroom somewhere, smelling like cock. They say they do this to every girl, but everyone I've ever talked to has managed to keep a guy for at least six months. Maybe it's something in their eyes—any time you turn on the radio, there's a song about how that first look does a dude in. The woman stares at the man, the man turns his head to the side, and just like that, the two are ready to shack up for eternity. I've tried to tell them that men are jerks who live to toy with your body, who grope you and stare at you and call you a slut until you bend over and let them stick their penises wherever they please, but nobody ever wants to hear it. They're too busy gossiping in the hallway about designer dresses and concert tickets and how if they buy the right perfume, they'll get Drake to marry them or something. All of the boys lick their lips when they walk by, but that doesn't stop them from batting their eyes and asking for flowers. My mom says it's a phase—girls can't handle the idea that they like sex, so they get the word out of their minds and replace it with *marriage.* Sometimes though, I think the marriage is just bait to get laid—boys get to tell their parents they're growing up, girls get instant access to boys' bedrooms and nobody ever asks them about the weird stains on their clothes again. They applaud our obedience, tell us we're being good little girls for doing things the right way, for waiting until we meet *the one* to take our shirts off and flash our tits. Whenever my girlfriends are with a new boy toy, they wrap their arms around them and look them straight in the eye, and you'd think they really are in love, that togetherness is a real thing. I wish I could act like that around men instead of being honest—that I could hold hands in the street and kiss in movie theaters and blush whenever they call my name, but I couldn't be able to pull it off if I wanted to. I'm too slutty, too eager to pull down my pants and shove that boy inside me. I don't like sex, but this is not about what I want. It's about getting them away from me. It's about giving them what they want so that I never have to talk to them again.

Beware the Armed Man

Beware the man who
who falls asleep with

a bottle of gin in his hands,
several boxes of ungraded papers,

who dreams of mansions
but instead wakes up to

homelessness, unpaid bills,
the threat of another child.

A wildfire already
on his mind:

nausea remedies, condoms,

lesson plans for a class
he wants, but realizes

he's not old or experienced
enough to teach.

The gardenias have seen
his kind before,

know the ache, but no one
in this city can hear them

above the empty noise of Android
and XBOX, megaphones,

morning meetings,
the disgust of a girl

who got a BMW instead of a Mercedes,

curling irons instead of straight hair,
last year's eyeliner, the wrong DNA,

who will be asked to go home
for no other reason than the fact that her

tops are too tight, she's
a little too pleasant to look at,

that she reminds her new teacher
just a little too much of where

he's been and not
where he's trying to go.

Beware the places that turn
inwards to pill bottles and vodka.

Beware the man who
wears his knife

on his tongue.

After Prom

I was a form without body:

oversized sports jacket,
a shit-stained hat.

At anyone's voice, I imagined myself igniting.

Me with a flask of vodka or a cigarette,
opening a bottle or flicking a lighter.

You said that anything can begin with a fist.

Should I have expected you to unhook
each bra strap, rip off my dress,

empty your semen into layers of bed sheets,
the seam of my mattress?

Imagine we never met, that what
passed for shadow between us

was not ours, but instead,
someone else's image of hair and nails.

I have tried to see myself this way--

unbruised lips and cheek,
a face with no black eyes.

You tell me that I can't
make love without light,

but darling, can't you see,
it's not that I'm shining,

it's that you're burning me alive.

Letter for K.

If I could write you a story,
it would be about the kind of thing that begins
with a fist-
Like the time you grabbed my throat
and pushed. Or the time you said that
you were born to live with your heart
in the clouds, away from flesh and voices,
and anything that could jilt you awake for a minute.
Mostly, it would be about the little fires
that harmed you every day:
chewing tobacco,
cancer scares,
the horseshoe circle of girls
who read a wedding out of the lines
in your palm, whose tongues could coax
any man into the language of *yes,*
who followed your shadow
into empty classrooms and bar fights,
then inevitably became shadow.
I could write you that story,
but it would begin the way it ends:
two lit cigarettes
looking for a place to burn.

Pyromania

Everything I touch catches fire:
boxes of baseball bats, the soot-stained jacket.

You ask me not to burn your image.

Pray for rain, for this blood and bone of me
to shape you into other things.

Daily, I try to learn the language of *fixed*--

undress drawers, iron out clothes meant for
garbage pails, the incinerator.

Any place my hands meet fabric,
the light from my body disappears.

Just once, I do not want to hear your voice out loud,
hear *fuck off* turn into bullets.

I want to imagine you as better than you were.

Pray for feathers, for this blood and bone body
to let go. Pray that you are already ash.

Carver

Between the reams of bushes
and monkey bars,

teenage boys playing football,
you wear your old life:

profanity-laced notebook,
a vodka-stained suit

and always, always
the ache of a girl.

From behind a clipboard,
you wait for her to damn you.

She hands out her pamphlet,
asks about *your god.*

You want to untether her,
destroy every religious symbol

that leads her to these myths.

You want to tell her
there is no burning man,
no heart in the clouds,

but if she lives, you'll regret it.

So you empty all of her into you,

her hellfire hair, her
straw, blood & bone arms,

empty her deep into your body
where no one, not even god, can see.

To My First Crush

If we were classmates, you would've hated my guts. I had the words and smarts, but you had baseball and girls and cheap vodka. Occasionally, you had me too— like the time I texted you naked pictures. Or the time I tripped on a pebble and accidentally fell in your lap. A woman in love shouldn't rely on tricks, but there was no other way you'd take me seriously. You told me I was cute, someone who didn't have acne or hangups about losing my virginity on the first date. Every time I'd ask though, you had a new reason you'd rather stay single—your aunt died, you lived too far off, you didn't own condoms. What made it worse was that my parents would give me shit for flirting with you-- groping me and smacking me and twisting my arms. By the time you noticed the red marks, you couldn't rescue anything. All of the criminals were out of my life, had already done their damage.

Break

It happened in the middle of a workout: the thud, the crunch, the sound of my slipped shoe-everything hitting the ground except my head. Nobody came to my rescue; and really, why should they, I've been drowning since before they got there.

In a nearby corner where no one could reach, the corner by the broken machines and the things labeled "Do not touch", a cell phone was ringing. I wanted to touch it, look for it, dig for it, because it was mine, and I had a feeling my mother wanted to pester me about my 3:30 appointment at the eating disorder clinic. Today was my first outpatient weigh-in and like a psychic, I knew I was disappearing. My sweatpants became hip huggers, my bras sagged and my shirts were so sweaty they might as well have been bleeding. Still, my mother said she'd be waiting for me, with a cake to celebrate my first month of recovery. It would have roses and flowers, everything the grocery store guy could possibly give away. I can still remember her in the kitchen, waving the big knife at me, the same one that's been my best friend for the past eight years, whenever I failed a math test or got teased at the bus stop.

I wanted to tell her, *it doesn't work this way, you don't just eat chocolate and get better*, but I'd be talking to the same woman who spoonfed me Snow White and Sleeping Beauty, who let me watch princesses get rescued until I fell asleep. When I was two, you see, nothing—almost nothing—could tire me. I cried and cried, violent, unprotected sobs, the kind of sobs I hear in the hallway every time a girl gets dumped. My parents drove me, cradled me, did whatever Doctor Spock or Phil—whoever came first—told them to do. Hell, my father even sang to me, in his raspy, cancer-ruined voice, sang Don Henley or Aerosmith or The Beatles, because those were the only songs he could mouth the words to. The rest were garbled, not understandable: wgen yu wsh upn ah str...

Nobody else in my family sang; they were writers and journalists, mathematicians and historians--people who taught in college, far away from eating disorders or exercise or men who got a rouse out of playing grab ass with a bunch of sixteen year olds. I've tried emailing one of my cousins, a guy who lives in Boston, by the name of Howard Zinn. My mother tells me he's pretty famous; she has his autograph and everything.

Sometimes, at 3 AM, I can hear her repeat the lines from his books, something about how life is a moving train, and nobody can be neutral. At night in the unit,

I've tried to picture it that way: the nurse's trays, the blood pressure monitors, the always spinning room.

It never works. Every time I stand up, someone knocks me back down, back to the place where nothing is touchable, where husbands beat their wives in between adjusting their oxygen tanks.

If I could write my cousin a letter, my big, famous cousin, who has a nice house and takes pictures with Ben Affleck, I'd tell him to build me a fort—no--a tower, away from treatment centers and illness and husbands who hit. I'd tell him that's where I want to live. Right there.

The Wreck of Your Life

Bipolar disorder
is like waking up with a hangover.
First come the apologies,
then the pink slips, the divorce
filings, the dead friendships
that turn cell phones into caskets-
When your first psychiatrist
assigns you your number
and finishes plotting the points
for a line graph that will document
the wreck of your life,
he will extend his arms,
just like a priest,
promising his own version of Heaven
in the form of white pills
and 12-step programs
that can melt *every sin*
off your drunk and helpless body.
Do not believe anyone
who tells you forgiveness
never comes with a jail sentence—
It is a cop
knocking on your door at 3 am

Below Heaven

It's 8 pm. My husband is massaging my ass, sliding down to my thighs, grabbing everything he can get his hands on. He tells me he likes it down there, where it's nice and soft. I just call it fat. We've been together for ten years and I still don't get why he's into me. I don't have a college degree, I'm not blonde, tall or particularly beautiful. Hell, if you believe the kids I went to camp with, I'm downright ugly, the kind of girl with love handles and a stomach and a million little acne scars that didn't want to go away. One particular boy liked to call me a fat slut when he got on the bus—right in front of the driver too, where all of the counselors could hear him. His voice still echoes whenever my husband touches me—the even tone, the way he makes sure to stretch each word out slowly and painfully across his tongue. In my mind, I tell him to fuck off, to go fall into a ditch somewhere, but he always finds something new to throw at me. Maybe I'm bad at sex. Maybe I don't know the way a man's body works—what to touch or play with, what to do to make my husband scream and kick and orgasm like the way the men do in the movies. Nobody ever teaches you how to be a woman— you just spend years failing at it and hope to god someone likes the act.

To My Almost Dead Friend

I want to think people are capable
of something that resembles love
but then I see your naked body
and all the places that surgeon
sliced your bleeding guts open
and it's hard to believe someone
who feels anything as warm
and compassionate as love
could willingly take a job like that—

suffocating organs,
sticking a knife into everything
that moves.

Animal

Sometimes, I feel nervous, like the minute I get out of bed, something terrible is going to happen. Maybe I'll die crossing the street. Maybe some creepy stranger is going to try to grope me on the subway. My mom says that it's normal to feel this way after you've been raped—the memory of having sex scares you to death, so you walk around with your fists up in case it ever happens again. Part of me wants to believe I can get over this—I'm tired of looking at strangers in the street and wondering whether or not they're carrying knives. It's been six years since it happened though. If I was going to be able to move on, I have a feeling it wouldn't take this long. Don't get me wrong—I realize that getting over things takes time, that you don't just wake up and feel like nothing ever happened. Even so, it's hard not to think I'll never be able to trust anyone again. There's too many bad things they can do to me—like steal my money or slip vodka into my drink when I'm not looking. My friends tell me I should worry less—just because one guy fucked me when I was drunk doesn't mean the whole world is out to get me, and besides, no one wants to be friends with someone who's paranoid. What they don't understand is that I can't get away from that memory. Every time I talk to them, my mind jumps back to something that he either said or did. Maybe I'm trying to make peace with it. Maybe if I replay it enough times, I'll be okay with what happened that night. My therapist says that the only way to get over something is to stop thinking about it. I feel like I should be more free, should be able to just put this away forever. Whenever I try to forget though, I only end up angrier at myself, for wasting so much time obsessing over what made this man want to tear my clothes off. I'd like to think he was just drunk, that there was no way he could've possibly done what he did without some kind of drug. Otherwise, I wouldn't be able to look at anyone without thinking they're vile animals who will do anything for sex. Never mind the fact that the guy apologized or that my therapist has been encouraging me to forgive him since the day I stepped in his office. He forced me to strip naked, to take all of my clothes off and kneel in front of him, like a dog. Nothing can make that okay. No matter how many times I talk about it or how many letters I write to him, I will always feel dirty. My therapist tells me that this will all go away if I just accept the fact that he made a mistake, but I don't want to accept it. I want to hold it in forever. I want to stay so angry that I never let anyone in again.

Chokehold

2 am and I am already drunk:
You're an alcoholic,
my boyfriend teases,
as he nurses the Guinness
that will inevitably turn him into
something I want to love
but don't recognize.
My mornings are always like this—
vodka bottles on the floor,
a mattress drowning in last night's puke
and the shame of an afternoon spent
trying to hook up with the man who
gave me my first black eye.
You think someone would have
grabbed me by my imaginary balls
after the first suicide attempt,
locked me in a chokehold and
yanked my naked body away
from the whiskey
and the wine and whatever else
I use to kill myself
while he gives blow jobs
to those old whores across the street.
When every day begins in a
blackout though,
the screams of the universe
could already be deafening

and you're just too shitfaced
to hear a goddamn word.

Whores Like Us

I think I'm becoming
the center
of the universe.
Strangers are
always spanking me.
Strangers are always
wrapping their hands around
my dirty little neck.
My friend tells me
it's normal for whores to
be violated like this,
that no one gives a damn
about a woman who
makes a life
out of getting raped.
Maybe I should quit
the sex stuff–
blow up my condoms,
marry some old blowhard
with six mansions.
All day, I have been
fantasizing about
what it would be like
to get naked
in front of my dad–
the wet breath,
the cum stains,
the small halo
of cigarette smoke
that leaves your mouth
after an orgasm–

The therapists will certify me.
The girls at work will say
how gross it is to
make out with the guy who
fucked your mom.
When you've been spanked
and beat and made a spectacle
just for being alive though,
you'll have sex with anyone
if means you never have to
cover your bra strap
or walk with a bodyguard
when you take the subway
back to your place at night.
You'll have sex with anyone
if it means you never have
to remember what it's like
to be human trash.

Bukowski Didn't Do This

I never want to wake up sober. I never want to trash the six packs in my fridge, to sign up for rehab and throw out the number of every single boyfriend who fucked me while I was shitfaced. There is nothing virtuous about quitting. Every time someone invites you to get smashed in a bar somewhere, your mind jumps to all of the different types of beer you guzzled, back when you were 21 and your professors didn't bat an eye if you showed up to class with whiskey on your breath. Even when the room spun, even when it got hard to stand up straight for more than five seconds and every building on campus looked like a big, shapeless mess. My brother says I should stop trying to defend my drinking—people who judge what I do are just looking for a place to take out their life's frustrations, and besides, it's easy to shame people when you're too old to remember what it's like to be reckless. For months on end, I've been doing everything I can to convince myself that there's nothing wrong with drinking—I swallowed a box of Tylenol. I drove back to my college town and got plastered in every single bar that had a happy hour. No matter how many blackouts I had though, no matter how many Jack and Cokes I downed or how many drunk men I coaxed into sleeping with me, some horrible fear always found a way to sink its teeth into my brain. Maybe I'm an alcoholic. Maybe my drinking is about something other than blind fun, and the reason my therapist is starting to give me dirty looks when I stumble into her office is that she's afraid I'll end up living in a jail cell if I don't seriously think about joining AA. Any time she talks to me about meetings, something in my body feels like it's being burned alive. Like someone tied me to a wooden post and threatened to incinerate my eyeballs f I don't puke up every single ounce of liquor in my body. All of my friends say I should ditch this shrink altogether— having a couple of blackouts a year doesn't mean you're going to ruin your life forever, and even if it did, nobody would ever think of me as anything less than what I tried to portray myself as. Clean and employable, a writer with two book deals. Any time I stop by on campus, some professor always asks if they can help me edit whatever I'm working on. Nothing I can do would ever make them see me for the human trash I am outside of class—not even if I were arrested in the parking lot, not even if there were a warrant out for my arrest and I got handcuffed right in front of their offices. Sometimes, I think it's normal to be a wreck if you make your living as a writer, that something about the idea of being famous makes people think they can act like they're above all gods. My friends think it has to do with the air—all the smoke we breathe in pollutes our brains, and we become so damaged that we can't tell the difference between what's good for us and what's going to make us die before we're thirty. I wish I could believe them. I wish I could shake my fists at the clouds and curse god out and act like whatever I do wrong can be blamed on something else. The fact of it is though, I'm the scum of the earth—the kind of woman who gets kicked out of men's house for smelling like booze, who will give a blow job to anyone if it means she has enough money to get to the liquor store. When you're as low and desperate as I'm getting, everything, even your own reflection, becomes a reason to get drunk.

Walking in Traffic

The day you left replays in slow motion—how you dropped me off in the middle of the street, how by the time I opened the car door, your eyes were already on the road. For months on end, we had been trying to get together. Did I become nothing to you the minute I said no? Every one of your exes told me you're a user—the kind of man who will say anything if it means getting a woman to pull your pants down and blow you right in front of the open windows, so that all of the neighbors can see you getting laid. I should have lost your number in the bar, should have had sex in with a stranger instead. At least if I were drunk, I could forget my mistake. Never mind the bruises on my legs, or the fact that I feel like a slut every time a man asks me to get naked. All of my friends have tried to convince me that sadness is a part of womanhood—they say it's normal to cry when you take your pants off, to fuck a guy and then wake up the next morning and wish it didn't happen. What they don't understand is that my life has been a slow and steady train wreck ever since I started dating—beer binges, bulimia, journals full of suicide threats. You were supposed to make me sober, to throw away the laxatives and the fatty foods and all of the other things that were stopping me from getting a job and growing up. Instead, you sweet-talked me into drinking and then bent me over so that you had a place to put your dick. Every morning I wake up, I pray that I'll forgive you, that I'll learn to love you and accept the fact that you've embraced your own demons, but there's no forgiveness for a man who sleeps with his students. There's only distance. There's only the ache of you walking away from me

For Doc

What ignites you is
the downfall--
rain, coffee, tooth decay,
cigarettes, a chalkboard's
vague suggestion of graffiti.
All day, teenagers will
tell you how easy it is
to disappear into the
language of the dead.
They will speak it with
their bodies, the way
a strong shove leads
to the threat of a fist.
Everything in your life
is resolved this way.
You try to ignore
the empty noise of a gun
in the window,
but violent men
cannot be disarmed.
They will reshape
themselves into murderers
and arsonists, and when
it's no longer newsworthy
to suffocate someone
with your bare hands,
they will create

new kinds of devils
for the world to hate.
When you reimagine
yourself as
their savior,
do not ask for
the advice of
your old gods.
There is nothing
more dangerous than
a man who disciplines
the world with a belt
wrapped around
his knuckle.

We Can't Stop

For the past couple of weeks, my friend and I have been sneaking out for beers. The bartender knows us by name, knows when we come and what we want. Hell, she even has it ready for us when we come in—lines up the Guinesses and everything. You'd think that somebody would kick us out—tell us to get a job and bum our liquor from the street, like every other broke college student, but we're the only ones who are keeping that place alive. I mean, maybe there are a couple of other schmucks who stumble in at 12 PM—guys with loose ties and shirts that barely fit over their pot bellies, who wreak of loneliness and whatever girl they slept with the night before, but they don't ever actually order anything. They just sit there and complain about politics or unemployment or why their wives are never home anymore. And it's real sad to listen to, but it's ruining me little by little inside, to think that that's what I have to look forward to when I get out of school. So I try to cover my ears or take our my iPhone—anything really, that would make you forget where you are or why you would want to be there. And I feel like between the booze and the texting and the endless amounts of music that come up, it should be enough, but something always leaks in—job search results or a phone call from an ex. My friend says I should try harder—find new music, join new groups—something, anything, that will keep my mind away from the fact that we're growing up. I've tried to tell him that it's inevitable, that someday, we're going to have to stop this party and learn how to pay rent and buy food and all those other things our parents do every day, but it just makes him drink until he pukes blood. Everyone I see on campus tells me that guy's going to be found in a ditch somewhere, and I'm going to join him if I don't take a cold shower and sober the fuck up. What they don't understand is that I don't want to be sober if it means making big mistakes, like losing a job or getting divorced. Those kinds of things take years to figure out afterwards–why it happened, what you're going to do next, and in between, you're ripping your hair out trying to decide what you'll need to sell if you want to keep your home. Maybe my classmates can take a life like that. Maybe they can hop from failure to failure and never lose a single tooth over it, but I binge drink until my mouth loses all feeling every time I think someone doesn't like me. There's no way I could deal with a mess up as big as that, let alone move on to something else. I've tried to expose myself to failure, to start a couple of businesses and take a couple of classes I wasn't good at. It only took away my appetite and made me afraid to leave my home without a bottle of wine in my hand. My mom says that I should keep throwing myself into different things—failure makes you grow up if you learn how to deal with it, and after all, nobody can be a little kid forever. Sometimes though, when the failures become big enough, growing up doesn't work. Sometimes growing up is just a way to disappear.

Note for Ray

I don't understand why my
ex loved you.
All he did was cut himself–
all he did was smoke and
fuck and drink himself into
the kind of bar fights
that end in a jail sentence.
Worst of all,
every scab resembled
a death sentence—
The way it blistered.
The way it burned alive
when a girl
crawled into him.
What is it about the
drunks that makes them
the envy of the world?
All day, I have been trying
to shape myself into
something lovable–
a pinup or a porn star
or a heroin addict with
daddy issues.
Even in your poems
though, they were always
one foot out of the deep,
dark rabbit hole life kicked
them into.

Never mind the fact
that they smelled
like poverty,
or that their boyfriends
were too busy
torching their bank accounts
to remember
what it is to sleep on
a bed of your own vomit—
they were relatable heroes.
the kinds of people who got
booted for drinking,
who will fry their
brain cells
in a power plant before
anyone ever figures out
what the hell it is we need
to talk about when
we talk about love.
Part of me thinks I should
trash your books already—
auction off the hardcovers,
make a campfire out of the
draft pages.
Nothing good can ever
come from the blind,
stupid business of taking
apart every book that crawls
into your closet,
and honestly, there are

easier hells a woman can
can create for herself
than the one that desecrates
the minds of the dead.

Funereal

The same daydreams
have been playing
in my head.
There is the one
where you disintegrate–
where your body
turns inwards to bars and
dark alleys and every hookup
ends with a noose
around your neck.
Afterwards, a funeral
march begs forgiveness.
Imagine classical music.
Imagine organs and fugues
and every single guitar
you've ever flicked
a cigarette at.
The world as you know it
is an impossibility.
Though you will shake
your fists at any anyone
who tells you *some sins

do not vanish withthe body*,
everything eventually
becomes an excuse for
drunkenness. For
bankruptcy and
homelessness and

the kind of life story
that could fit
in a gutter.
This is how you disappear–
with a Guinness
in your pocket and
the vague memory
of a young man
turning into ash.

Every Last Detail

I don't know what I'm becoming anymore. I don't have a social life. I don't have a job or a boyfriend or any of the things that someone my age is supposed to have by the time they get out of college. All I do is just sit in front of my computer for hours and hours on end, checking my email and googling all sorts of useless things that no one should have enough free time to care about. What makes it worse is that I can't even remember what made me want to know these things in the first place—my parents don't talk about them, my neighbors don't come to my door and say that my future is going to be completely ruined if I don't find out every last detail about the way the world works. It just pops into my head when I'm laying in bed at night, trying to think of something that would be boring enough to drown out the constant suicide fantasies that creep into my head when I'm alone. Like the ones where I take too many happy pills. Or the ones where my parents find me hanging from a noose in my bathroom, unable to speak or breathe or tell them what made me want to throw away the rest of my life. My therapist says there's nothing wrong with me that I could ever pinpoint—some people are just born sad, and no matter how much you try to talk them out of it, there's nothing good enough to make them decide to stay on this earth. For months, I've been doing everything I can to dig myself out of this deep, dark rabbit hole I've been living in—volunteered at a homeless shelter, smiled at coworkers. No matter how many kind things I did though, no matter how many people I helped or how many times I saw someone hold the door for a total stranger, there isn't a cell in my body that believes people are any good. Maybe I'm a bad person. Maybe there's something wrong with my genes that makes me unable to feel happy, and the reason I spend so much time online is that it's the only place where I can find anyone who loves me. My parents say I'm in love with it because it's fake—there's no worrying about having to see someone's face when you tell them something they don't like, and they're not in your life enough for it to hurt you when they leave. I wish I could believe them. I wish I could go online and start a conversation with someone and come away thinking that person means nothing to me. As soon as I get away from it all though, I grow sad and empty inside, and the only way I'll feel alive again is if someone else pays attention to me. Sometimes, I think I need to throw out my computer, that the only way I'll ever learn how to talk to real people again is if I stop going online altogether. I mean, maybe it would be hard the first couple of months. Maybe I would shake and sweat and get nervous inside the first time I go outdoors. But if that allows me to talk about my real problems, if it allows me to explore what gives me panic attacks and makes me think about killing myself, then I think it's worth it. When you're as lonely and miserable as I am, anything, even pain, feels like a vacation.

All the Celebrities Do It

Some random stranger
emailed me last night—
asked me my tit size
if there was any chance I'd let
a 31 year old virgin
what a woman looks like
with her bra off--
Here I am,
two months out of a
relationship with
a married man
and already, the opposite sex is
asking me to get naked.
Maybe I should go the porn
route--
snap pics of myself when
I'm masturbating,
pay some middle-aged douchebag
who's got a fat wallet and a photo
of himself smoking weed with
Amanda Bynes
to remake the internet
in my naked, cum-soaked image.
It wouldn't be the classiest way
to make myself famous--
Mothers will stalk my apartment,
Feminists will wave their fingers in

my face
every time I take a dump in a
public bathroom.
But when you're as poor and
desperate and hungry as I am,
you'll let anyone see
what you look like naked
if it means they
will know who you are
when you die.

Crystallized

I can't stop reading my ex's old text messages. All the stuff about how we were going to have kinky sex in his apartment, or how I was the only girl he ever wanted to see naked. My therapist says it's a way to heal—I can't understand why he dumped me, so I obsess over these things to see what I did wrong. The problem isn't that I don't agree with her—it's that I was never in love with the guy in the first place. Don't get me wrong—he had a couple of good things going for him—like his love for sports or how his clothes were snug in all the right places. As soon as we were done fucking though, I would zone out and look the other way, like he didn't exist. My friends say I'm afraid of falling in love. Maybe they're right. Maybe the only reason I'm so into sex is that I never have to worry about men rejecting me. For months, I've been trying to get myself to be more open with people—wrote them poems, expressed my deepest, darkest secrets over the phone. None of it ever worked. It just made me feel worse about myself, for having done so many things wrong in my life. And I mean, I guess that when you talk about yourself enough, you learn how to deal with who you are, but until that happens, you're stuck reliving all of the worst parts of your life. Parents who beat you, men who only love you when you take your clothes off. My therapist says that the only way I'll ever be able to get over the hurt is if I work my way through it. But if getting over it means never wanting to see my ex again, I don't want to be healed. There's just too much I'd miss about him, too many weird and crazy things he did to make me happy that no other person would ever do for me. Like how he kissed my neck, or how he liked to suck my toes when we made out. And maybe my guy never got on his knees and gave me a wedding ring, the way all boys are supposed to when you fall in love, but that doesn't mean he isn't into me. It means he doesn't want to commit right now. It means he's just as afraid of falling in love as I am.

Blame the Princess

In my daydreams,
he tears my pants off.
In my daydreams,
he rams his dick
inside my mouth
and suffocates my throat
and tells me it can't be love
until someone dies.
For hours on end,
I think of burning my
own womanhood,
of lighting a cigarette
and incinerating
every organ in
my overly sexed body.
Whatever I touch
smells like shame.
There's vodka on my
bra straps, on my thong,
on every crinkled dollar bill
I cup in my palms–
Someone should have
married me off
by now–
Grabbed onto my money
for dear life and
bought my way into

picket fences and dogs and
a house with enough
diapers to make
any housewife dizzy.
No matter how many men
I coax though–
no matter how much
I tease them or how many
places I walk around
with my shirt off,
no one will ever bat
an eye at a woman
who's still naive enough
to know when
she's been raped.

Dear Lover

When I look at your picture, I think of everything wrong you ever did to me. Every black eye, every night I went to sleep and wondered if someone would find me in the morning, with a phone cord wrapped around my neck. All of my friends say I should get rid of you—no good ever comes from dating a man who doesn't respect your body, and if things stay the way they are now, they'll be burying me before I have a chance to realize I'm powerful enough get out. For months, I've been trying whatever I could think of to get rid of my old life—packed a suitcase, opened the window so I could get a glimpse of the bus stop. As soon as I take one step toward the door though, I feel your clawing at my feet, like the thought of not having a woman in your life is enough to kill you. Maybe you don't know how to exist by yourself. Maybe years of living with your mom left you so needy that there's no way you'll ever be able to figure out how to take care of your own body. Even if I showed you how to boil pasta, even if I took you to the post office hundreds of times, so that you can see how to pay a bill, there's no way you'll ever do it if there's no mother figure to hold your hand. My therapist thinks I should love you more—that if I kiss you enough, hug you hard enough, indulge every single want and need in your little head, you won't need to act out to get attention anymore. The problem isn't that I don't want to spoil you—it's that I have too many things going on in my life to make you happy. And I'm not about to give up my kids or my teaching job or my million dollar book deal just because you're too sad to get out of bed. You wouldn't either, if you had the chance to be rich and famous. You said so yourself, the day our eyes met at the bar—how much your writing meant to you, how hellbent you were on making it big. What happened to the man I talked to that night, the one who asked me about my books and my kids, who didn't care if he had to wait five hours for me to read his little love notes? Every night, before I get the last beer out of the fridge, I relive our relationship, down to the moment you decided to punch me into the ground. None of it makes sense though—not the way I want it to, not in a clear-cut way that shows where you stopped loving me and started becoming a drunk monster who throws me against the wall every time I do something you don't like. All of my friends are becoming alarmed at the bruises too—at how big and purple they look, at how even after months and months, they won't go away. And I guess those spots are god's way of saying that this relationship isn't right, that even if you have no clue how to take care of yourself without me, I shouldn't die trying to dig you out of your own grave. Dear lover, I have thought about this goodbye over and over, in so many different ways, and there is no easy way to say it. So I won't say it. I'll just tiptoe out of the house when you're not looking, and you can call me when you learn the difference between your head and your ass.

Politics as Usual

Every time I talk to
the world,
it belittles me–
Even when I burn
its pants off,
even when I grab the skin
folds of its neck and turn
everything between us
into ash–
All of my friends think
I should sweet talk
my way
into fucking,
that nobody will ever love
a woman who asks to be
slammed into walls.
They don't understand
how hard it is
to fuck someone when
your body grew up in
violence though–
you stroke it and play
with it and call it pet names
and just when you think
you're horny enough
to sext the hot piece of ass
on the next block,

some criminal idea
sinks its teeth in your brain,
and it's like watching your
dad all over again—
down to the part where
he slides his dick
into your young
and awkward hands
and threatens to beat
the ever-loving shit out
of your vagina.
You think someone
would've taught us all
how this ugly business
of living is supposed
to work by now—
slipped us a manual
or a lab guide, anything
with paychecks and
picket fences and all of
the nice little toys we
have sex to get our hands
on in the first place.
No matter how much
I research though—
no matter how much
I channel surf or how many
news stories I flip through
on my laptop,

someone always needs
a woman
to strip down to
her thong and ask
to be tied to a
stripper pole.
Someone always
needs a woman
to skin alive.

Note for Henry

It is 5 am and
I am pretending
that you're not dead.
There's booze on the
fridge, in my bag,
in the dark recesses
of my booty call's truck--
Neither of us will get
tanked enough to
forget our bodies,
but I guess once you
get outta college, it stops
being fashionable
to wake up in your vomit.
Don't get me wrong--
I know women are more
likely to blow strangers
when they're shitfaced,
that old, horny men
like you have made
a career out of fucking
the kind of girls who
wouldn't know Home
if it snuck up
and bit 'em in the ass.
With all these TV whores

making a spectacle
out of everything that
crawls into their
vaginas though,
it's hard not to wonder
why anyone has sex in
the first place.
All my friends tell me
to masturbate,
to tear my pants off
and play with everything
I can get my hands on.
Any time I think my
body is smart enough
to orgasm though,
something makes the
room melt and
turn inwards,
and I begin to realize
how sad it gets,
when a bastard like you
could die without knowing
what it is to be in love.

All Sparks Will Burn Out

I think I met that guy last night. The guy who buys you the dress, who slips the big ring on your finger and then tells you how you're unlike any other woman he's seen naked. I never thought people fell in love that fast, but as soon as he flirted with me, everything in my body felt warm and fuzzy inside, like I didn't care about who I was or what I was doing with my life anymore if he wasn't in it. My friends think I should call him—any guy who makes you fall in love that fast is worth checking out, and besides, there are too many good lovers out there for me to spend the rest of my life alone. For hours on end, I've been staring at his number. I feel like I should pick up the phone, should leave a text or at least a facebook message saying how crazy he made me in bed. Every time I think about him though, I get all nervous inside, that he just wants me for my body and nothing I say or write down will ever sound smart enough to convince him I'm more than that. Don't get me wrong— I like the feeling of being touched, of having a man shove his dick inside your mouth and tell you you're no good for anything if you don't know how to blow him. Just once though, I wish the guy would kiss my forehead and treat me like a real girlfriend when the sex part is over. Maybe they can't love me. Maybe I'm so good at knowing how to get them off that they don't care about what I think or feel. My therapist says I should stop fucking men on the first date— men like things they have to work for, and they're not going to call back if I've already given them what they wanted. Sometimes, I think I should stop dating altogether—ditch the bar scene, delete every number off my iPhone. If I go a week without sex though, I feel sad and empty inside, like I'm a stupid girl who doesn't deserve love. And I guess that's what happens when you grow up in a house where your parents blame you for everything that's going wrong in their marriage—where they hit you and beat you, where they spank your bare ass just because they can. It doesn't stop me from believing that I'll fall in love though—it just makes me more determined, to find the guy who's going to undo all of the bad stuff my parents did to me. Even if we fight all the time, even if we scream at each other and spend our whole lives talking about how getting married was the biggest mistake we ever made, it would be worth it if I have someone who will hold my hand when I'm dying. It would be worth it if I don't have to go to that big upstairs place alone.

One of Those Boys

I'm reading a love poem
and watching two men hit
each other over the head with
a chair. There is the threat of
a murder in everything: tables,
ropes, baseball bats, barbed wire,
the body's imagination of a knife
in its tongue. Whatever is touched
turns to ash. Imagine blood lights.
Imagine every fist invites the
possibility of a funeral. All alone,
I retrace the outline of my bruises.
Though it has been two years
since the last restraining order,
I still cannot undress without
feeling as though I have been turned
into something unrecognizable.
Scratch marks on my vagina,
two metal objects carving their
geography in each nipple.
Each time I describe the story,
I am performing my own unraveling.
The signal to war is not yet over.
My brother insists on watching
wrestling because it is a kind of
catharsis. He wants fists. I want
to forget what it felt like to burn

alive. Every time someone turns
on the stove, part of me wonders
if my head is going to be lit on
fire. It has taken me forever to
understand that this is not a
normal way to fuck. No one
in their right mind would ever
hurt a complete stranger for fun.
I have tried to tell my brother
this night after night, every time
someone on TV throws another
man into a wooden table and
a pool full of barbed wire,
but with all these big,
wet dreams he gets about
putting someone in a chokehold,
I just know my brother
will be one of those boys
who joins a wrestling league
who kidnaps a woman
who will kill his wife
before he learns how to speak
a language other than hate.

Disappearing

I no longer want this
unhappiness, this blood-
bleached body's suggestion
of a knife in the throat.
Everything in my flesh
imagines some radical act
of disappearing. There
are cigarettes on the rug,
the carpet. A hug is
its own funeral. Do not
trust the warmth that
is already invested in
the politics of *more*:
More whores, cars, cigarettes,
gas money, more poems promoting
the spectacle of the dead.
At work, there is constant
discussion on which two women
will be raped in a dumpster.
I do not say that I know
what it is to be fondled.
This only makes its happening
more inevitable. In my mind,
I am preparing for the act.

For naked bodies, for the random
metal object flirting with my clit.
It cannot scare me that I am going
to be unraveled. One out of three
women eventually find out what it is
to be sexually assaulted. If I am
lucky, the man will be a stranger,
not a friend, not someone I have spent
months talking to, not the
all-american I fantasized about
taking to my parents in high
school. I want the menace to
coax me into invisible languages.
Things that know no literature,
no scrawl in the back of a police
report. His appearance will not
be a nagging ache. Will not repeat
the nightmare of my old suicide
attempts. My body no longer
understands terror.
I am all stone.

A Shot at Sanity

I flushed my crazy meds down the toilet today. Stuck my middle fingers down my throat, puked up every ounce of lithium that boiled in my blood. Everyone at school says I wanted to kill myself because I wasn't getting laid enough—girls who wait too long to lose their virginity become so obsessed with sex that they can't think straight, and the only way they can ever have a shot at sanity is if they empty their cabinets and swallow anything they can get their hands on. For hours on end, I've been doing everything I can to explain to them that I don't care about sex—I threw my vibrator out. I slammed their bodies against the lockers and threatened to murder them if they ever called me a slut. No matter what I told them though— no matter how many black eyes they woke up with or how many curse words I mouthed in their ears, some horny little shit always thought up a new way to insult me in the hallway. Maybe I was born drunk. Maybe my mom was too busy putting away tequila shots to realize someone knocked her up, and the only reason she never aborted me is that I gave her another excuse to mooch off the government. Sometimes, I think I should spike my coffee when I wake up in the morning, that I will never be able to get out of this world alive if I don't start learning how to be okay with the idea of showing up showing up to class drunk. Even if my parents got in trouble with liquor, even if they lost big jobs and got kicked out of mansions, there's nothing on their arrest records that could make me wanna trash my fake ID, no amount of eviction notices or pink slips that could ever be sad enough to stop me from drinking myself away from everyone. My mom says she'll send me to a psych ward the minute I show up hung over—call the fire cars over, tell them to fire up the sirens and everything. She doesn't understand how growing up around an alcoholic will make you want to black out though—every morning now, the minute I step into homeroom, my teacher will go on and on about how it should be illegal to make people go to work sober. There are too many deadlines, too many people giving you shit about little things that won't be important five minutes from now. It's enough to make anyone get hammered, to steal someone's credit card and buy the first bottle you can lay your desperate eyes on. Sure the world will hate you, sure you'll be slapped in the hallway and have to spike your tea with vodka just so you can live look at yourself when you get undressed in the morning, but when you're as surrounded by booze as I am, there's nothing more gratifying than waking up in the morning and feeling so hung over that you don't remember what you did yesterday. There's nothing more gratifying than being able to forget.

My Boyfriend's Closet

A room full of clocks
and none of them can tell time

A shoebox full of animal corpses
and no shovel to bury them

A man dressed in his mother's clothing
and no teenage boys to call him a faggot

A secret wrapping its naked hands
around my dirty little throat

It Must Go

I think I'm dating a married man. Every time he gropes my
ass, he looks down at the floor, like the fact that we fucked
is some big secret he wants to tuck into the back of his
mind. And it doesn't matter how many times I touch him
on the shoulder or pet him or stroke his hair—there's
always something guilty about the way he closes his eyes
when he shoves his dick inside me, something about his
body language that knows he's sleeping next to someone
who shouldn't be there. My friends say I should ask him up
front the next time we have sex—when people sleep
around, they just assume everyone thinks they're single, so
they'll be surprised enough to answer honestly when
someone asks if they're taken. For months, I've been
thinking of ways to end it—I wrote him a breakup letter. I
sent him emails telling him how much I respect him. No
matter what I said though, no matter how much I smiled or
how many times I shook my head, just to say that I hated
what he was doing, he always found a way to make me
look like the bitch. Maybe I used him for sex. Maybe he
had an abusive childhood, and I'm one more reason he
thinks about cutting himself off from the world forever. My
friends say it's not my role to find out—our hurts are
always more important than whatever is going on in the rest
of the world, and as long as someone does something to
make us feel bad, we have the right to leave them out in the

street to die. Every time I walk into my bedroom, I relive the nightmare of being the other woman—cum-stained sheets, the wedding ring that slid off during a blow job. You think that would be enough to make me drive to his house and dump him, right in front of his wife and his kids, but no—I take his calls and cancel whatever I have going on in my life, just so that he has a place to put his dick. My therapist say that I should do whatever I can to make sure I can't contact him–married men like that pray on young girls who don't feel good about themselves to turn down sex, so they'll overwhelm you with text messages until you agree to let them treat you however they want. She doesn't understand how hard it is to ignore someone like that though. You put your phone on vibrate and block his email address and just when you think you've cut him out of your life long enough to forget he exists, his last message pops up right in front of your face, and suddenly, you're reminded of all the people you've ever hurt in your life. I wish I had the guts to put my feelings away forever, to just blank out and conveniently forget the fact that I kissed this miserable human being in the first place, but the fact is, love doesn't work that way. It sinks its teeth into us. It tears our bodies apart, inch-by-inch, and turns us into the monsters our parents promised to protect us from.

Aches

All day, I am coaxed
into bar fights. Into
whiskey and weed and
the kinds of doors that
turn inwards to bad men.
Everything is a reminder
of how much of me has
disappeared. Outside,
I measure my loss by
the number of bullets
in each window. Every
dream reimagines
the image of my corpse
in some strange man's
backyard: the dress,
the glass slippers, the
way my voice catches fire
when it yells *rape*.
Death has its own music.
All afternoon, my tongue
imitates a casket.
I want to believe that
anyone can remake death
into something completely
and stupidly harmless.
Ever since the text

message that landed my ex
a prison sentence,
it has gotten easier
to convince myself
that the body does not
know the difference
between a black eye
and a knife in the
gut. There's proof
in your bones.
Believe me when
I tell you that
life is nothing
but an anatomy of aches.

This Body is a Cage

I think my hair is
starting to turn white.
Any time I lift up my sweatshirt,
to give some hopeless fuck
with a 20 dollar bill and a crack pipe
the strip tease that will
lead him to kick his kids
into a drug den
and divorce
his old shrew of a wife,
the same old ugly reminders
sink their teeth into my scalp
and bite me in my bleach-blond ass-
that I am weathered,
that years of drinking
and fucking and listening
to sad music
has left me pale and
damaged enough
to look like
everyone's grandma.
You think someone
would buy me a box of dye
or something–
a carton full of wet, hot ink
so that I won't have to

murder my own body
just to convince myself
I'm still young enough
to live forever.
Even if my hair was
jet black though,
even if I streaked it and
straightened it
and incinerated
the last bits of my scalp
with a hot iron,
everything
I look at
when I look at my lovers
would still be a painful reminder
of how
we are all
deeply
and beautifully fucked.

What I Call Life

Someone mugged me
on the subway.
Someone tore my bag open
and ripped out every single
condom they could cup
in their palms.
What made it worse,
nobody even
gave a damn enough
to make a spectacle
out of the dark, hot
semen pit
that is my sex life–
Sure people threw
shit at me.
Sure people grabbed
onto their children
and mouthed bad
curse words
every time I motioned
like I was going to get off.
But there was
no murder
in it,
no strange pleasure
in the fact that

anyone with tits
and a brain
can now become
a porn star.
if a woman's privacy
is a thing that needs to be
raped,
the least you can do
is flirt with us
while we're naked
and on fire.

Pussy

You write about as well as I did
when I was six–
with your use of animals
and your need to make
every goddamn
thing you write
in the shape of an animal-
My friends think I shouldn't
hate your guts,
but they're nice people.
They don't know what
it feels like
to look at a poem
and want to
gouge your eyes out
with fire.
For months, I've
been trying to forget
you exist.
I trashed my library.
I attacked my computer
with a blowtorch.
Every time I got in bed
to write or fuck though,
I thought of your bad words
and your bad sex
and it's no wonder
a woman like me would

say such angry things
when the literary world
is contaminated
with men who
can't fuck,
can't write.

When You're Manic

Anything that comes out
of your mouth is an insult—
a fat lip, a fist,
the ache of an ice pick
in the back of my brain.
At all hours, I have
watched you unravel—
one hand on your clit,
another reaching for
the beer bottle that
will turn everything
into fists and black eyes
and whatever else
passes for abuse
between alcoholics at 3 am.
Tell me how no married
woman leaves this world
without a knife in her throat.
With your bra unhooked, it is
easy to think of you as victim.
Your trouble begins with
the aftermath—
how lucid you speak, how
nothing, not even your hair,
will ever smell like shame.

Is there something about
the act of sleeping
with animals that makes
you want to live on impulse?
Every morning, my bathroom
repeats the sound
of you flushing your pills.
You said they were
interfering. You said
I was a hindrance, the world
was a hindrance, that
no one, least of all a
slew of white men in lab
coats, should have to know
how many men you've sucked off.
More than once, I tried
to practice the art of distancing—
to ignore the condoms, the
trashed beers, the chewing tobacco
under every chair.
There is no horror like
the house that opens itself
to strangers.
To stay alive, I repeat the
myths my friends have drilled into me—
that there was a mixup
at the hospital, that you were
someone else's, that this criminal
in my living room is not
my daughter
my daughter
my daughter.

Been Caught Stealing

I'm thinking of shoplifting again. Even if the cops rape me, even if they tear my clothes off and bend me over, just so they can inspect the tag in my thong. Everyone at school says I'm doing this because it's the easiest way to get a man to touch me—no cop in his right mind would want to have sex with a fat girl, but it's part of his job to frisk anyone who breaks the law. For months on end, I've been watching them strip whatever they can get their hands on—babies, grandmothers, the women who smuggle thongs in their bras. There's something exciting about watching a man strip you naked, about being pinned against the wall and having complete strangers shove their dicks in your mouth. Never mind the fact that what they're doing is illegal, or that every little boy in that store can see the cum stains in your jeans—you've become the kind of woman who can get any man to blow her, who will never go home at night without a damp, hot body wrapped around her arm. You think my friends would be happy I'm getting laid, that they'd applaud how up front and frank I am about what I want from the men who ogle me. Instead, it's all finger wagging and feminist lectures about how sex isn't something you just give out. Whenever my friends start talking about marriage, I feel like trashing their womanhood, like kicking them to the ground and fucking them until their vaginas bleed. Sure they'd hate me, sure they'd throw me out of their houses and tell me never to call them again, but when everyone calls you a slut just because you want to have sex before marriage, you begin to resent the fact that we all have to deal with this ugly thing called womanhood. My therapist says I should learn how to feel comfortable with talking about my own nakedness before I start fucking strange men—people aren't used to dealing with someone who chooses to be promiscuous, and it's easy to get offended if everyone labels me for doing what I do. She doesn't understand how hard it is not to be violent around my friends though—I look down at my phone and check my text messages to see who's gonna be my booty call tonight and just when I think I'm comfortable enough with my own choices to ignore all their insults, someone says something about how my mother was a slut, and suddenly, it's like we're all in a wrestling match, down to the part where I tackle them to the floor and pull on their hair. You think someone would tell me not to sleep around if I'm not comfortable with it, to delete my phone numbers and tell these men not to talk me into sexting them anymore, but I guess when you're the kind of person who shoplifts just to get men to rape you, there's no amount of good will that can make people stop shaming you on Facebook and apologize for throwing rocks at your home. There's no amount of charity that can make people love you.

The Assault

This woman in the living room
is not my mother.
All day, men have been
carving their private aches
into her tits and her spleen
and every other place
the deadbeat I call my
dad has threatened to
suffocate with
his bare hands.
The neighborhood says
it's normal for the cops
to fondle you, that they
won't know a woman's
been assaulted unless
you tease her open
with a cattle prod.
For hours,
I've been thinking
of every way to
electrocute a body.
If I had balls, I'd spank it.
If I had sociopathic
tendencies, I'd stalk its
girlfriends and
plant a bomb under

every single toilet
it'll ever take a dump in.
Even when my dad
used to grope me,
I'd fantasize about
the noise a dead
body makes when
it gets smacked by
concrete–
the crunch, the thud,
the hope, then
embarrassment
of a blood-soaked shoe.
Anyone with a knife
and a brain can unravel
human flesh, but
until a stranger
rapes your mother
at gunpoint,
you will never know
what it is, what it really is
to kill someone.

Ball and Chain

Saturday afternoon and there's a baseball game on every channel. My brother loves it—says it's a release, that it stops them from thinking about grown up things, like work and school and how the hell they're going to get the money for rent at the end of the month. And I try to nod sympathetically, to tell him this growing up thing is hard on everyone, but ever since he went to high school, his life has been one big party. Sneaking bottles of wine from the kitchen, making passes at complete strangers. Every time he opens the door, I'm afraid of what he'll bring home next. My parents tell me it's a phase all boys go through—they drink and smoke everything, have a couple of one night stands, and just when you think they'll be like that forever, they'll put on a suit and tie and tell you they're ready to get a job. I should feel relieved, should throw my hands up and let him do what he wants, but I'm his older sister. I'm supposed to be the one who protects him from hangovers. I mean, maybe they're right. Maybe he'll get off the couch and realize that he's wasting his life on booze, but until then, I have to be the one who holds his hair back and bends him over, so that he doesn't choke on his own vomit. I don't like doing this—I'd much rather be getting wasted in a bar alone. It's nowhere near as much fun to destroy yourself that way, but at least my family wouldn't have to watch me slowly unravel over the course of months and months, with no hope of looking into treatment or at least admitting I have a problem. When he's sober, my brother tells me that this isn't the way to go, that I should move out and learn how to be happy some other way. The problem isn't that I don't know how to be sober though, it's that I don't know how to die. Don't get me wrong—I've thought of leaving him behind, of just ditching him and hoping someone will find me collapsed in a bar somewhere, but every time I sneak out the door, I start to shake and cry, like a pathetic little sissy who's afraid of her own shadow. Sometimes, I think it's a sign—that I'm supposed to live until I'm seventy, get married, live behind a nice picket fence with a nice wife and have nice kids. Right now though, I'm too scared to figure out what it all means. There's just too much about drinking I don't know or understand—like how some people can stay sober for as long as they want and others threaten to punch something if they go a minute without booze. And I mean, I guess I could google it or read about it in a book somewhere, but I don't have the money or patience to learn why people kill themselves. So I sit in the living room, alone, with the remote in one hand and an open beer bottle on the table, and I pray that at the end of this, all of us will still be alive.

Womanhood

The first time I tried
to kill myself,
I was 14.
Knives drenched
the kitchen counter,
the bathroom, the cum-
soaked spaces where
my cousin fisted his way
inside my naked body–
Any time I took
my clothes off
to masturbate to a magazine
or play with my nipples,
whatever I got my hands on
began to turn to ash.
You think someone
would've cleaned out
the apartment by now–
called the police or
a religious figure,
somebody with
fists and balls
and a mouth
big enough for
the deep, dark embers
that every little boy who's ever
seen me naked calls

my womanhood.
Instead, it's all cigarette
smoke and blow jobs and
the kind of nagging hangover
that won't quit until
it sinks its teeth into
every fabric of your body.
Whenever any boy
threatens to tear
my clit open,
my teenage self will try
to talk me into
the suicide attempt
that will set my organs on fire–
For hours on end,
I'll browse for things
I can unravel myself with.
No matter how much
I down though–
no matter how many pills
I OD on or
how many guns my
fingers set off,
some local doctor
will always be evil enough
to keep a wall between
me and that
big upstairs place
where all men become sexless
where all women become
untouchable.

Battles

My mom says that if I just stop starving myself, I'll be able to appreciate all of the little ways she shows she loves me—like the way she cuts my turkey sandwiches into the shape of a heart, or how she absolutely double checks to make sure the chocolate milk is right at the front of the fridge every time I go to grab a snack. Whenever I'm standing near the kitchen door, any place remotely near that damn door, it stares me down, coaxing me to just take one sip. Don't get me wrong; I love chocolate milk, but I mean, those things have about as much fat as a porterhouse steak. There are other things that will hold me 'til I see her again—Budweiser or Heineken, weed, blow, whatever will allow me to forget my name or why my mother can't keep a job for more than three weeks. She tells me that drugs are for people with no self-control, but this is coming from a woman who raids the entire fridge before she says *hello*. Even my three-year-old sister knows better than to eat an entire pack of raw cake batter or drink two bottles of coke, straight up, without reaching for anything that remotely resembles a glass. You can smell her as she's doing it, too—the sugar, the syrup, the weird mixture of spoiled eggs and shame. Everything in the fridge is gone in three hours, but hey, she leaves me the chocolate milk, that one little reminder that I used to be kind, that I had a childhood and a body that didn't betray me. Sure, my teammates at soccer practice pretend nothing's changed—they cheer me on and tell me how amazing I look, running and jumping and kicking things, but after every game, they're all sitting together, whispering about how my thighs jiggled on that last save. What kills me the most though isn't the phony oo-rah spirit; it's the hugging, the kissing, the play-by play-talk. Any time parents start watching, some little boy is guaranteed to run after them, in tears, over whatever he did to cost his team that game. If I were his mother, I'd put my coat around that boy, massage his shoulders and kiss each cheek. I'd tell him how lucky he is, that the only battles he ever has to fight are outside.

Macy's

A woman walks by the dressing rooms, past the designer pants, past the perfumes, past the two million oversexed high school girls who will buy anything if it means they're not going home alone tonight. She picks the ugliest shirt off the discount rack and holds it up to her body real close— like it's some kind of armor in case one of those girls drags her into the bathroom and sticks her head in the toilet, the way they used to do back when she was their age. The whole school would hear her kick and scream and curse, and after about a month of this, it became a routine, to watch this girl unravel until she ran home, crying, with her head covered in toilet paper. You couldn't put that year into words, or the sudden shame that comes with seeing her in the back of the store, alone, with her three-sleeved shirt and her shit-stained hair, so you walk far away from her, far enough that you can't smell her or trace the scabs on her forehead. The further you get though, the more lost and stuck she looks, like a teenager who never figured out how to grow up. You pray for one of the salespeople to walk her out of the store, to direct her to her car, to point her to any direction other than the one she's going, but they don't do any of these things. They just point and laugh to each other, whisper thanks to god that they're not her.

An Ugly Act

I cheated on a quiz yesterday—
ripped my bag open,
grabbed every textbook I could get
my hands on—
None of the other guys asked me
about my ugly act,
and why would they—
this cheating business,
it's a way to prove your manhood,
a quiet acceptance of the fact
that you grew up with a dick
and an anger problem
and you know how
to beat right and wrong
into something unrecognizable.
All of the presidents steal their speeches.
All of the news reporters build their books
from the blood and bone of Wikipedia.
Hell, even my dad,
before he became the guy who will happily
talk to strangers about
the virtues of capital punishment,
snuck a couple of law books into his desk
the day of the bar exam.
Now, I'm not saying
everyone has

the balls to be like this—
there are those who will tell you
they have never cheated,
never shoplifted,
never tried to sneak into a bar
with a fake ID.
But when so many others
are brutally honest about how
they fucked their way
into the job of their dreams,
it gets hard not to think
that humans as a whole
are nothing but
lawless
animals.

PTSD

When he's horny, my pet guinea pig likes to bite the girls' cage. He's only about two pounds, but his teeth can gnaw through just about anything—DVDs, furniture, you name it. My boyfriend says that breaking things is just an animal's way of trying to flirt, kind of like the way he used to flex his biceps whenever he saw me crossing the street. All of the other girls would go crazy over him--squealing and blowing kisses and fanning themselves. You think they'd be able to find someone else to hit on, but I guess it's easier to flirt with a guy who's already taken. There's no date, no attachment, no having to worry about what kinds of girls he's talking to at work or when he'll stop returning your calls. Every night is the same ritual—brush my teeth, get undressed, check his phone for calls from her. We've been together for four years and not once has he ever come home with another girl's smell on his breath. I should let this go, should accept that he doesn't cheat, but that's not how I deal with things. I throw plates on the kitchen floor, scream at my pets and curse myself out for ever getting into a relationship. I lock myself in my room, all alone, and leave my boyfriend to clean up after the demons in my head.

Coax Me Into Leaving

Your body is a mess of stars.
For hours, I've tried to burn it,
to scald it, to torch
all the places
my hands found flesh.
No matter how much
I unraveled though--
no matter how many
wastelands I sunk my
teeth in or how many
times I tried to tease
your organs apart with
my damp, hot breath,
everything was still
an excuse for black eyes.
All morning, I have counted
the dead on my mattress.
The human body is nothing
if not a gross display
of old aches.
In my sheets alone,
I have found scabs, hymen
blood, the aftermath of
a scratch on my cheek.
This should be enough
to coax me into leaving,
into shacking up

with strangers and
pawning my phone
for the first plane ticket
out of the deep, dark rabbit
hole you've threatened me
into with your fist.
But any woman who fucks
an animal
will never be able
to slip high heels on
without digging into
text messages and asking
security guards to stalk her
when she gets on the bus
in the morning.
She'll never be able
to walk without
a noose around her neck.

Last Act

I'm going to rehab on Saturday. My friends say I don't need it, but
if I keep drinking the way I am now, I won't be able to go five
hours without feeling like I'm going to die if I don't get some kind
of wine in my blood. Shaking and sweating, walking into walls.
Part of me thinks that I was born to get hooked on this stuff, that
something went wrong with my genes, and now the only way I'll
ever be happy is when I self-destruct. Then again, if drinking a
bottle of Merlot every night was so good for me, I wouldn't wake
up in a pool of my own vomit. I'd be like my husband, breaking
tables and strangling everyone who said something that hurt me.
And I guess that kind of violence scares people, but that's because
they don't know what it's like to fall in love with a man who beats
people up for a living. Every time I walk into the house, there's
always some kind of threat. Maybe I'm going to get my head
bashed in the wall. Maybe I've been terrible in bed, and the only
way my husband can get back at me is if he ties me up and then
puts me to sleep. My friends think I should leave him—anyone
who's that into fighting will look for any excuse to hit you, and
besides, you don't want your son to grow up knowing that his dad
was a wife beater. What they don't understand is that men are
supposed to behave this way. They're supposed to lie and cheat and
make you so miserable that the only time you'll be able to look at
them is when you're drunk. At least, that's the way it's always been
when I'm in a relationship. The guy starts out promising 89
everything, but as soon I'm done sucking his dick, he'll do
anything to get rid of me. Never mind the fact that I cook and clean
or that I quit my business job just so that I could watch him get hit
over the head with a chair. I'm the old bitch, the one who lost her

looks the second she started popping out kids. There's nothing good I can do to please him, no way to keep him from hitting on the twentysomething girls who walk around the wrestling ring with their shirts off. And anyway, I was one of them once. I knew how good it felt to watch men drool over me. Still though, it burns me alive when I think of all the things he's probably doing to those girls as we speak. The way he touches them. The way he makes them feel warm and excited all over. It's enough to make me file the divorce papers right now, to walk out and take my son, to tell my husband I don't want to have to drink to be happy anymore. But that would mean learning how to be alone, miles away from the fake lights and the screaming fans and the men who fawn over me because I'm The Crippler's wife. Even if I wanted to, I don't know if I could figure out how to live without his fame. There's too much I hate about myself, too many mistakes that would haunt me every time I go outside. All of the bad men I've dated, all of the times I let my husband scream at me and didn't say anything. In the back of my mind, I realize I'll have to talk about this stuff when I go to treatment, that someone is going to ask whether my husband gave me that black eye. But I don't want to say anything that would put him behind bars. He'll kidnap my son. He'll tie me up, then strangle me with his bare hands.

Abusive Lover

Sometimes, in my dreams, I still see you.
It is just like when I was a teenager and
thought you were god—
Only this time, you are sober.
When I lean in, I don't even smell it on your breath
or on your clothes,
and this is almost enough for me
to trust you with my body,
but I don't.
I remember waking up with black eyes.
I remember looking at my fists and
wishing they were shotguns.
Your drunken rages have made me
fear all men.
Every time I have sex, I wonder
if this boyfriend will be the one who makes good
on your promises to unravel me forever.
There is no amount of violence that can undo the shame
of loving a man who beats you,
but it feels good to say it out loud—

I'm glad you're dead.

Thoughts During a Hug

I am tired of being
untouchable. Tired of
cigarettes, of six packs
and crack pipes and
the wastelands of
human flesh.
Every year, I have tried
to reimagine myself
in a stranger's image.
Whatever passes
between us
turns to shadow:
our tongues, our
notebooks,
the body's false
suggestion of death.
At all hours,
I smell the threat
of a black eye.
Think of rough sex,
how easy it is to
brutalize a woman.
Behind a writer's desk,
you have coaxed
yourself into an
imaginary violence.
Everything turned

inwards to sword fights
and funerals and the
invisible suicide of a man
inhaling meth.
In my mind's eye,
it is easy to imagine
you as something
monstrous--
your cigar pipe,
your baseball hat,
the way every teenage
girl disappears into
your arm. My first lover
made his existence into
a spectacle. Seven years
later, I still cannot
look up to
another man without
imagining the horrors
of his flesh. All of his skin
cancer, all of the places he'll
ask me to rub his cum
when he jerks off.
If your idea of *hello* is
rape, incest, the vague
ache of a knife on
the tongue, then there
will be nothing between us.
I have no interest in violence.

I only speak the language
because no one has
ever melted the icicles
around my heart.

Other Lives

There is the fear
of murder in my body.
At all hours,
I have imagined knives,
baseball bats, the
window's suggestion
of a bullet. Whatever
gets touched becomes
unrecognizable:
my dog, my husband,
my nightstand, my laptop,
the Facebook post that
explained my unraveling.
Strangeness is
a necessity.
In public, I am always
disappearing into
other lives.
I want to believe
that a manic episode
can be written
into nonexistence.
Even during daylight,
my corpse is careful
not to study its shadow.
You say that this bodily

violence was an
inevitability, but after
a rape, nothing, not
even logic, can help you
appreciate
how gone you are.

At My High School Reunion

I am nobody:
a wife, a stranger,
the vague suggestion of
a one night stand in my
breath. All night, the men
imagine smothering
me into their cigarettes.
There is no harder
trick than disappearing.
For months,
I have been a voyeur
inside the wastelands
of strange men.
Every time I touched flesh
became an empty invitation
into condoms and crack dens
and the empty puff
of an after sex cigarette.
Any other woman would
have killed herself in strange
and inscrutable languages--
a lock on the computer,
seven virtual trash bins
for every illegally downloaded
picture of child porn.
Even in tenth grade,
it was easier to turn

inwards than acknowledge
how every shouting match
ended in a fists.
My home life followed
this hollow narrative:
threats, black eyes, the
nightmare of a knife near
my bed. When you imagine
what it is to sleep with
monsters, do not
include the part
where you
attempt suicide
in his basement.

Regrets are a
thing with teeth.

Your Ex-Lover is Dead

I had that dream last night. The one where he can't move, the one where he falls asleep in a pool of his own vomit and doesn't wake up. My mom says it's because I got sober—the only time we ever hit on each other was when we were drunk, so now that I can't go to bars with him anymore, it's like our whole relationship is going to die. For months, I've been trying to get him to do this with me. I threw out the wine bottles. I sold the thermoses he hid his booze in. Every time I tried to convince him he had a problem though, he just spat in my face and told me what a bitch I am, for making him give up the only thing that gets him out of bed in the morning. Sometimes, I think I should just move away from this guy—that no matter how much I want to clean his clothes and pay his bar tabs, he won't get why he needs to put the booze down as bad as I do. Forget the fact that he gets arrested a million times a year, or that his teacher friends tell me they can smell the vodka on his breath when he comes into school. He pays his bills on time, and as long as he can do that, he sure as hell isn't going to throw out the six pack in his fridge. It's too calming, too big a part of his life to swear off forever. If he goes a couple of hours without getting tipsy, his hand shakes so bad he can't write. Maybe he can't quit. Maybe his whole body is hooked on this stuff, and he'd kill himself if he tried to go a day without drinking. My friends say anyone can get off it if they want—they just have to admit they can't have it, that the only thing alcohol does is fuck up your life. I want to believe them. I want to believe that a guy like my ex can just wake up one morning and never have a drink again. But with the way that guy acts when he's buzzed, I won't be surprised if he's getting his brains bashed in right now. Some guy will look at him funny, some bartender will shortchange him five cents on his fifth jack and coke. I've been trying to block it out, to forget the horrible feeling that comes with knowing someone who will die before he ever gets to do anything good in the world. Even when I'm in meetings though, it's hard not to feel guilty, that I got off the booze and he's still stuck in his old bar scene, hanging out with women who know exactly how to use him. They pretend to flirt. They promise him ten more drinks if he lets them crash at his place for the night. As soon as he starts buying flowers and calling them "the one" though, they block his number. You'd think someone who's spent his whole life getting drunk would figure out how this works, that he would at least know better than to chase after people who never learned how to love. But I guess if he knew that, he wouldn't be drinking. He'd be going to rehab with me. He'd be holding my hand and telling me how good it feels to be alive.

The Day I Wrote My First Short Story

A baseball shattered the
glass in my window.

I tried to wash the rug off,
clean the room with my bare hands,

but any place I tried to touch,
little shards would pierce my flesh.

Cups cracked.

Dolls' heads broke off,
splintered into plastic bits

that got stuck behind radiators
and wood drawers,

compartments too small
for any human finger.

As I stuck my hands out
to reach for a broom,

several gashes opened
along the soles of my feet.

I clotted veins
with my palms,

watched skin
fall away from bone.

Hollow

If you believe my mentor, he learned to write from a book of short stories one of his college professors gave him-not the gunshot wounds, not the invisible ache that lingered for years and years after he tried, and failed, to kill himself. Sometimes though, I'll find little notes in between the chapters of whatever he's editing-things like 'got out of jail today' or 'what a loser' and I can't help but wonder if he's injecting a little bit of himself in there, if he got raped or beaten like the people in the stories, and writing those things is just his way of working it all out. I guess what I'm trying to say is, I'd like to know if anyone, in this horrible mess called life, is really capable of writing fiction.

Why No One Becomes a Writer Anymore

Poems are like bad men—
drunk, unstable, always threatening to ruin you
with their fists and their guns--

Poems are like desperate men—
broke, idealistic, always trying to wrap
its politics around your dirty little throat-

Poems are like the worst men you will ever marry—
the ones who carry their rings
in their asses,
who will fuck anything with tits and fishnets
and enough money to call them a cab at night—

Do not let anyone convince you
that poetry is dignified—
It fucks you in dumpsters.
it rapes you in front of teachers
and classmates
then breaks your vagina open
with whatever it can get its hands on

and the worst part of
all of this--
worse than the rape,
worse than the embarrassment

of having the ugly boy in the back
know what you look like

when your vagina is bleeding,
is no one will tell you
that you've been violated.

Fences

Everything holds
the image of skid
marks. Of fists and
gunshots and the
window's repeating image
of a knife in the throat.
Was there something
in the nightclubs
that convinced you to
flush your wedding ring?
All night, I have retraced
the outline of our photos.
I want to be that bride
again and again.
This grotesque
scrutiny is enough
to murder any human being.
All night, the neighbors coax
their own narratives into
tabloids, TV fodder, the news
crawl at the bottom of
a midnight infomercial.
A celebrity can coax any
woman into silence with the
gold in his wallet. How much
did you offer the teenager who

blew you? I want to know
what misfortune will disarm me
next. Tell me how many
lawyers I will need–
what you will rob me
for, how many houses
I will have to sell for food
money. The world has
made my life into a spectacle.
Sometimes, at night, I
wonder if I am secretly the
real-life version of the poor,
black woman in that
August Wilson play.
The one who raises her
husband's love child,
but kicks him out the minute
his eyes attempt to coax her
into the language of
forgiveness. I don't remember
the name of it, but what
I do remember is my strange
empathy for her when
every phone call invited
the possibility of a love-child.
The way the room shrank,
the way all of her
clothing began
to smell like a stranger.
It is not good enough

that the world
is burning you alive.
I need to be the wife
who smashes your windshield,
torches your suitcase,
who says, without
opening her mouth, that
you are a womanless man.

Dead Languages

I am the world's plaything.
All day, I imagine its damp,
hot breath on my forehead,
the way everything turns
to shadow. The body that gets
raped knows no embarrassment,
no wet shame, no repeating
threat of a knife in the throat.
Whatever opens its mouth
invites me into dead languages.
Consent is either invisible
or not taught. All day,
the mind recreates a
narrative of its unraveling.
First, there are the manias.
Then, there are the drinking
binges, the blackouts, the
bar room doors that close
inwards to strange men.
After each failed attempt
to shape me into something
unrecognizable, my brain
will find new ways to coax
the rest of my broken body
into prison. It has been like
this since the first time a man
groped me in public. He spat.
Or cursed. The act was not
important. Neither was his

flawed morality. At the end of
the deep, dark rabbit hole
the world calls life,
we are nothing
more than a sum of
the bodies
we've touched.

For a Girl

My camera studies the
outline of her–
how many dolls
in each shirtsleeve,
her mouth the only thing
big enough to navigate
the geography of silence
between us. The employees say
it is always like this on day
one–your awkwardness an initiation
into the play world of the children
you are hired to supervise.
In the babysitting room,
there is the music of action
figures and baseballs,
two boys simulating a custody
battle over someone's toy train.
Every house becomes a container
of small voices, each one of them
operating under the assumption
that any day now, someone's parents
will give them permission
to inherit the world. Even though
none of them can pronounce it,
they already know the meaning
of politics, how in the middle of
a handshake, the brain

will inevitably
invent its own language
of lasers and knives and whatever
else will coax this other
human body into magically
vanishing. I was that age once.
I understand what it is to be
strong and frighteningly impulsive.
In pictures of my childhood self,
the shadows suggest a narrative
of temper tantrums and plots and
the quiet need for something,
anything that would eliminate
my brother. The guilt still nags
at me from time to time. The guilt
of hating, of learning to evaluate
the world through the lens of my rage.
Emmalee, if you are reading this,
do not believe your mom when
she tells you all strange men
turn into monsters. There is
no evil. There is only
a toxic misuse of the imagination.

Your Rumors Are True

"I'm seeing my teacher."

The words fell out of my mouth like a pair of loose teeth. For months, I had been trying to put it off, to give myself a reason it would work out. Every time the words entered the back of my tongue though, they stayed there. My parents would try to coax it out of me. They would pry and prod and check my clothes for semen. One time, I even caught them smelling my shirts—pressing their noses against the fabric and everything. Dad said he needed to do it for my safety, but who was he kidding—I had lost my virginity to the entire football team years ago. Everyone in school knew about it too—it was a grade-wide rumor, the kind of thing that gets passed down and passed down until even the red-headed freckly kid in Math class starts throwing paper planes at you and calling you a skank.

There was no way I could live down my reputation in front of my parents—and even if I tried, they could see the cum stains on the back of my shorts. Still though, as I pointed to all the places my teacher had groped me, it was hard not to imagine my dad drop kicking that guy in the balls. Ever since the incident on the bleachers, he'd been promising that he would be my protector, that any time a boy gave me trouble, all I needed to do was go to him and that kid would end up in a corner crying somewhere, without dirt or makeup or anything that could cover a black eye. I should have told him the first time my teacher grabbed my ass, but my dad was always out in a bar, too busy enjoying his beer and whatever hot chick was checking him out to care about my small problems. He even threatened to take me out of this world once—flipped me over on my backside and whipped me with his belt. Most of the scars faded within a couple of months, but there was always something left over—a bump on my thigh, a chipped piece of skin on my forearm...

The day before I graduated high school, my teacher gave me my first and last massage.

Muscles collapsed. Black and blue marks from my dad's beatings began to spread out, disappear into my legs and thighs until I couldn't see them anymore.

As his hands got lower and further away, he looked down at me and smiled, and I knew we would never have each other again.

Before a Suicide

If I could, Amanda,
I would beat my fists

against the things that harm you:
vodka tonics, pills, heroin,

a cigarette's dark embers.

I would feed your disappearing flesh,
sear skin together,

massage light back into the places
you've learned to hide from uncomfortable aches,

from sex, from the wildfires of men.

Any place I touch,
you burn alive, Amanda.

For years on end, I've watched
you empty yourself-

toss beer bottles into street corners,
lay your head in some new lap.

I want to find you,
feel for your breath.

I want to tell you that death is not this
slow indictment of the self,

but you are already
too gone for platitudes.

So I'm learning to retreat
instead, Amanda,

retreat into my silence,
my books, my sleep.

In our bedroom, your last puff
revisits my neck
like a lost stranger.

I open the window,
watch your body

explode into stars.

Acknowledgments

I would like to thank the entire Fictionaut literary community for their consistent support and feedback as I undertook this project. Sam Rasnake, Gary V. Powell, Gary Hardaway, Bill Yarrow and Beate Siggriddaughter particularly stand out in my mind.

I would also like to thank the English faculty in CUNY Queens College, for helping me edit drafts of the material in this book.

The following poems contain borrowed material:

"Letter for K"—

one phrase from "Thirteen Attempts at Saving My Soul"
by Beate Siggriddaughter

"Violence, Interrupted"—

two lines from "Issac, After Mount Moriah"
by Saeed Jones

"Before a Suicide"--

one line from "8 AM"
by Joani Reese

About the Author

Amanda Harris is a Master's candidate in English at CUNY Queens College. Her poetry and fiction are featured in *Olentangy Review*, *MadHat Annual*, *Camroc Press Review*, and *Black-Listed Magazine*, as well as other fine places. She currently resides in New York, along with her parents and brother.

Praise for *Rage*

Warning: Amanda Harris's writing inflicts cuts and bruises. Her stories leave you feeling a little like you've engaged in voyeurism, stolen something, hurt someone, or been hurt, and enjoyed it more than you should have. Reading this collection is like binging with your buddies Bukowski and Carver, stumbling and roaring from bar to bar, telling lies and starting fights, pissing and screwing your life away, and waking up in a room painted the color of train-wreck regret. Amanda Harris will make you remember things you don't know, like how good it felt to sleep with the cute, young teacher all the other girls just talked about doing. Like the time you got off on reading sexy texts from your ex. Like lying to your therapist, your siblings, your friends, and then wondering why they don't trust you. Like going for Erica Jong's zipless fuck with that married guy from work or deciding not to eat the turkey sandwiches your mom cuts into the shape of hearts. This is edgy, gutsy work. This is the real deal, kids. This hurts so good.

--Gary V. Powell, author of *Lucky Bastard*

Rage, the new collection of poetry and flash fiction (Miscreant Press) by Amanda Harris, is a book of grit and edge. Work after work exudes a clear and unapologetic voice the reader can't help but follow: "the broken thing I am learning to love," "no burning man, / no heart in the clouds," and "there's only the ache of you walking away". The writer is at war with the missing part – the missing answer to life – the truth that "disappears". These poems and fictions are meant to disturb, fracture, jolt, and they do so with vigor. Harris is unafraid of the torn landscape she creates, and that makes *Rage* an impressive read.

--Sam Rasnake, author of *Cinema Verité*

* 9 7 8 0 6 9 2 4 8 1 2 0 2 *